1. One of the last of the unsuccessful Messerschmitt 210, built before production ceased in the spring of 1942.

2. A Junkers 88 of Kampfgeschwader 76 on the Eastern Front;
note the unit's hornet emblem. (Hallensleben)

WARBIRDS ILLUSTRATED NO. 6

The LUFTWAFFE
1933-1945
Volume IV   ALFRED PRICE

a&ap

ARMS AND ARMOUR PRESS
London—Melbourne—Harrisburg, Pa.

Introduction

I should like to extend my grateful thanks to those kind individuals who allowed me access to their private collections of photographs. Without their support many of the photographs in this sixth volume in the Warbirds Illustrated series would have remained hidden from the general reader. Each photograph has been selected for its interest to the enthusiast, the modeller and the historian and, as in previous volumes, no attempt has been made to follow any cohesive historical theme.

Alfred Price, 1982.

Warbird 6: The Luftwaffe, 1933–1945, Volume IV
Published in 1982 by
Arms and Armour Press, Lionel Leventhal Limited,
2–6 Hampstead High Street, London NW3 1QQ;
4–12 Tattersalls Lane, Melbourne, Victoria 3000, Australia;
Cameron and Kelker Streets, P.O. Box 1831, Harrisburg,
Pennsylvania 17105, U.S.A.

British Library Cataloguing in Publication Data:
The Luftwaffe, 1933–1945. – Warbirds illustrated series; 6
Vol. IV
1. Germany – Luftwaffe – History
I. Title II. Price, Alfred III. Series
358.4′ 00943   DG635.G3
ISBN 0-85368-514-2

3. Junkers 87Bs of III/StG 77 returning from an attack on a target near Sebastopol in the spring of 1942. (Schmidt)

Layout by Anthony A. Evans.
Printed in Great Britain by William Clowes, [Beccles] Limited.

▲4 ▼5

6▲

4, 5. A Henschel 123 dive-bomber of I. Gruppe Sturzkampfgruppe 165 based at Kitzingen in 1937.
6. Line-up of aircraft at the seaplane station at Hörnum in 1937. The aircraft on the left are He 59 torpedo bombers belonging to 3. Staffel of Küstenfliegergruppe 106; those on the right are He 60 seaplanes of 1./KüFlGr. 506. (via Schliephake)
7. Dornier 17E bombers of KG 255 based at Memmingen, pictured in 1937. This unit was later re-designated KG 51. (via Selinger)

7▼

8. LZ-130 Graf Zeppelin, the second airship to bear that name and sister ship of the ill-fated Hindenburg, flew several electronic intelligence-gathering missions for the Luftwaffe during August 1939, immediately before the outbreak of war.

JU 87B

▲9 ▼10

DO 17P

10

11▲

9. A soldier keeps a watchful eye on a Ju 87B of Stab. StG 2, photographed early in the war.
10. Do 17P reconnaissance aircraft of Fernaufklärungsgruppe 22.
11. Generalfeldmarschall Hermann Göring congratulating men of I./StG 77 at Radom, Poland, on 13 September 1939. Other senior officers in the foreground are: second from left, Generalmajor Baron Wolfram von Richthofen, commander of Fliegerkorps VIII, of which StG 77 was part; fourth from the left, Generaloberst Erhard Milch, Inspector General of the Luftwaffe; and, fifth from the left, Generalleutnant Hans Jeschonnek, Chief of Staff of the Luftwaffe. (Scheffel)

▲12

12. Crewmen of III./KG 76 stationed at the forward airfield at Lovet snatch a meal between missions during the campaign in France. (Unger)
13. A Do 17 of III./KG 76 lies with its back broken after battle

damage had forced the aircraft to make a wheels-up landing at Lovet. (Unger)
14. An attack on an enemy column during the campaign in the west in 1940, viewed from the nose of a Do 17.

▼13

1

▲15 ▼16

15, 16. Dornier 17Zs of III./KG 3 being prepared for a mission during the campaign in the west.
17. A bomb strike by Ju 87s of I./StG 77 on one of the ships evacuating troops from Dunkirk, 1 June 1940. (Schmidt)
18. Aircrew of I./StG 77 inspecting a French column they had earlier attacked near Auxerre. (Scheffel)

▲ 19

19. Junkers 87Bs of III./StG 77, during a practice formation shortly before the Battle of Britain. (Bode)

20. A Messerschmitt 110 of I./ZG 26; during the Battle of Britain this unit operated from St. Omer.

21. A Messerschmitt 110, probably belonging to ZG 26, taxiing

out to take off from an airfield in North Africa.

22. Members of 8./ZG 26 pictured in front of their Messerschmitt 110, which carries the unit's emblem on the nose.

23. A pilot of 7./ZG 26 about to board his aircraft.

▼ 20

21▲ 22▼ 23▼

▲24 ▼25

24. Junkers 87B dive-bombers of I./StG 2, probably photographed in the spring of 1941 at about the time of the campaigns against Greece and Crete.
25. A snow-camouflaged Ju 87B on the Eastern Front, probably in the winter of 1941/42.
26. The unit badge of 9th Staffel of Kampfgeschwader 76 is

clearly visible in this photograph; the Dornier 17s of this low-altitude attack unit were fitted, unusually, with a 20mm cannon on a flexible mounting in the nose. (Raab)
27. A Do 17 of 1./KG 76, bearing the unit's 'little devil' emblem, undergoing an engine change at Langendiebach. (Rehm)

▲28 ▼29

▼30

31▶

He III

28-30. German ace pilots who fought in the Battle of Britain.
28. Pilots of JG 2, from left to right: unknown, Hauptmann
Helmut Wick (killed in action against Spitfires of No. 609
Squadron on 6 October 1940), Oberleutnant Rudolf Pflanz
(killed in action on 31 July 1941), and Oberleutnant Erich Leie
(killed in action on 7 March 1945).
29. Hauptmann Josef Foesoe (left) describing a combat. Among
the group is Leutnant Erich Hohagen (on the right, wearing a life
jacket). Both pilots fought with II./JG 51 during the battle and
survived the war. (via Ring)
30. Hauptmann Wilhelm Makrocki commanded the
Messerschmitt 110 unit I./ZG 26 during the battle; he was killed
in action during the attack on Crete in May 1941.
31. A Heinkel 111H releases a stick of SC 50 bombs.

32. Dornier 17s of KG 76 accompanied by Messerschmitt 110 escorts – zig-zagging to maintain station in the background – pictured over England during the Battle of Britain. (KG 76 Archive)

33. Unteroffizier Günther Unger of 9./KG 76 at the controls of his Do 17. (Unger)

34. Hermann Göring congratulating men of I./KG 76 who had just received spot-promotions for flying the largest number of missions during the Battle of Britain, Beauvais, 18 September 1940. From left to right: Göring, Major Schweitzer (Gruppe commander), Oberfeldwebel Mairose (promoted to Leutnant), Feldwebel Carstens (to Leutnant), Unteroffizier Sobol (to Oberfeldwebel) and Oberleutnant Hallensleben (to Hauptmann). It was one of the rare occasions when Luftwaffe personnel were promoted for this reason. (KG 76 Archive)

35. Senior Luftwaffe commanders pictured during the Battle of Britain. Left to right: Generaloberst Hans Jeschonnek, Chief of the Air Staff; Generalfeldmarschall Albert Kesselring, commander of Luftflotte 2; General Speidel, Kesselring's Chief of Staff; and General Bruno Loerzer, commander of Fliegerkorps II, which was part of Luftflotte 2. (von Lossberg)

▲36

36, 37. The debris of war. **36.** The burning wrecks of two He 111s, one of KG 1 and the other of KG 26, which came down close to each other near Lydd on 11 September 1940. **37.** A Messerschmitt 110 piloted by Oberleutnant Rudiger Proske of I./ZG 26, which crash-landed at Lydd on 18 August 1940 after being attacked by Squadron Leader Don MacDonnell of No. 64 Squadron.

38–40. The spoils of war. Squadron Leader David Lloyd, the senior fighter controller at Tangmere, leaning against his car (**38**) as fuel is syphoned into it from the tanks of a Junkers 88 of 4./KG 54, shot down by his fighters during the Battle of Britain. Appropriation of ex-enemy property for private use was forbidden, but Lloyd felt he had as much right to the petrol as anyone else! (Lloyd)

▼37

38▲

39▲ 40▼

▲42 ▼43

44▲ 45▼

41. (on previous page) Arado 96 trainers from the pilot training school near Paris, February 1942. (Wiegand)

42–43. The night blitz on Britain, 1940 and 1941. **42.** A Heinkel 111 pictured taking off carrying two SC 1000 Hermann bombs under the fuselage. **43.** Fires burning on the ground in London, as seen from one of the German bombers. (via Dierich)

44, 45. The Allies did not pose the only threat to the German raiders. **44.** A Junkers 88A-5 of KG 1 which ground-looped after returning from a sortie over Britain; landing accidents at the ill-equipped airfields in France and Belgium were a frequent occurrence in bad weather. **45.** A lucky escape for the crew of an He 111 of KG 55, which ran into a balloon cable during an attack on Bristol. The cable sawed its way through to the main spar of the wing then, fortunately for those on board the aircraft, the wire broke. (via Dierich)

46. Ground-towing an early production Focke Wulf 190 fighter at Marienburg in the summer of 1941.

47-50. A selection of photographs from the album of ex-Major Helmut Bode, commander of the dive-bomber unit III./StG 77. 47. Bode (left) in conversation with the fighter ace Oberst Werner Mölders in Russia, shortly before the latter was killed in a flying accident in November 1941. 48. Bode in his Junkers 87, bearing the Gruppe emblem which was based on his family's coat of arms. 49. Bode's Ju 87 pictured in the spring of 1942 during the operations against the Soviet fortress at Sebastopol. 50. The fortress of Sebastopol under attack.

▲47 ▼48

▲51

51. Ground-running the engine of an FW 190A-3 of III./JG 51, one of the first units on the Eastern Front to receive this type.
52. A Zwerg (dwarf) hot air heater is used to warm the engine of an FW 190 prior to starting. Such equipment was necessary during the harsh Russian winter, if the aircraft were to be

maintained at readiness without frequent engine starts.
53, 54. Junkers 87Bs of III./StG 1, photographed at a forward landing-ground near the River Dnieper in Russia, probably during 1943. Note that the aircraft in illustration 54 has had the streamlined 'trousers' removed from its undercarriage legs.

▼52

▲55 ▼56

55. A Junkers 52 operating on the Eastern Front.
56. Ground crewmen easing an aircraft engine out of the main freight door of a Junkers 52. The inability of this aircraft – by far the most numerous in the German air transport fleet – to load and off-load bulky objects was a major limiting factor in German airborne supply operations.
57. Behind the front. A Junkers 52 fitted with a magnetic ring used for exploding magnetic mines from the air. The ring was energized by current from a generator driven by an auxiliary motor in the fuselage. (via Schliephake)
58. Oops! A spectacular accident at Cracow in Poland, caused when a Messerschmitt 109 of the Cracow-based training unit Ergänzungsjagdgeschwader 3 and a visiting Junkers 52 from the flying school at Puetnitz tried to land at the same time in the same place.

me 210

▲59 ▼60

59–62. Rare operational photographs of Messerschmitt 210s of III./ZG 1, one of the few units to use the type in action. Taken when the Gruppe was based in Tunisia early in 1943, they come from the collection of ex-Leutnant Fritz Stehle (**60**), who served with the unit. The Me 210 was soon found to have dangerous shortcomings and was withdrawn from operational use.

61▲ 62▼

▲63 ▼64

65 ▲

66 ▲

63–68. Photographs from the collection of ex-Oberfähnrich, later Leutnant, Helmut Wenk (65). **63, 64.** An FW 190A-4 of IV. Ergänzungs (operational training) Gruppe of Schnellkampfgeschwader 10 based at Cognac in France in May 1943. After training, in the summer of 1943 Wenk was posted to Crotone in southern Italy, where his unit II./SKG was engaged in operations over Sicily. **66.** Wenk taking off from Crotone on 1 August 1943 to attack the Allied munitions dump at Nicosia in Sicily. His aircraft, one of eight engaged in the attack, carried one SC 250 bomb and two 66-gallon drop tanks. **67.** The operations post of II./SKG 10 at Crotone was idyllically situated under a cork tree; by this stage of the war Luftwaffe installations in the area were liable to suffer sudden and devastating attacks by Allied bombers, hence the need for concealment. **68.** A close shave for Helmut Wenk: blinded by dust from the aircraft in front while taking off from Crotone on 27 July, he swerved off the cleared area and struck a tree to one side of the airstrip. The aircraft careered away, shedding both wings, both drop tanks, both undercarriage legs and the bomb. Wenk escaped with a severe shaking.

67 ▲   68 ▼

▼69 ▲70

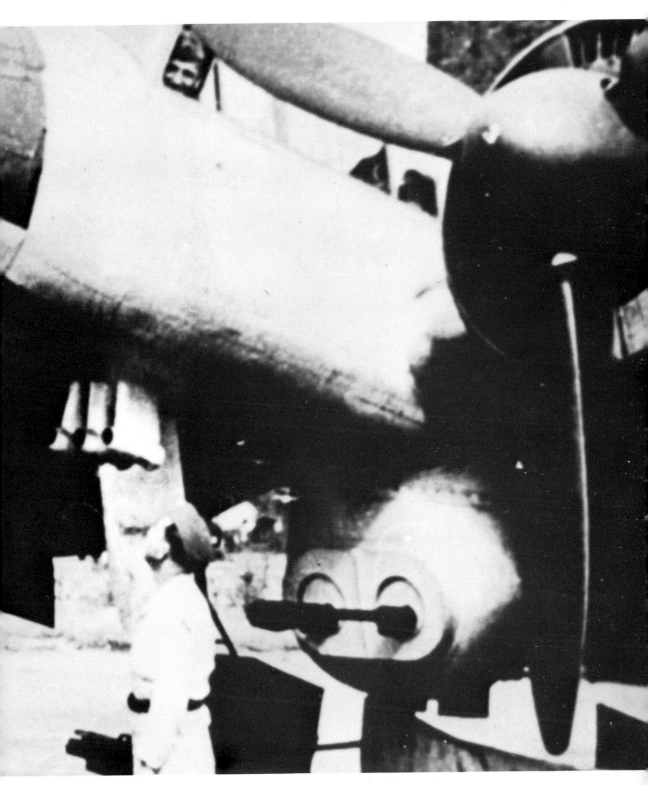

69. A close-up of the nose of a Dornier 217N-2 night-fighter, showing the armament of four MG 151 20mm cannon and two MG 17 7.9mm machine-guns, and aerials for the FuG 202 Lichtenstein airborne interception radar. (via Redemann)

70. An experimental installation of two MK 103 30mm cannon in a semi-trainable installation under the fuselage of a Junkers 88P night-fighter. The three pipes under the cockpit were intended to give an organ-like note in flight, as a means of identification to flak units on the ground; the method was not introduced into general use. (via Aders)

Ju 88

He 177

▲72

▲73 ▼74

75▲

71. (on previous page) A Junkers 88 T-1 high-speed reconnaissance aircraft of Fernaufklärungsgruppe 123, pictured at Athens-Tatoi in 1944. (via Roosenboom)

72, 73. Although it has the appearance of a twin-engined aircraft, the Heinkel 177 bomber had four engines – two coupled to each propeller. This arrangement was one of several novel features that gave continual trouble when the aircraft went into service. Both illustrations show He 177s of II./KG 100, which received the type in 1944.

74. An He 177 of I./KG 100 which took part in Operation 'Steinbock' – the series of attacks on London and other cities in Britain early in 1944.

75–77. He 177s of KG 1, which re-equipped with the type in 1944 and for a short time used it on operations on the Eastern Front.

76▲ 77▼

▲78 ▼79

78. Until the final stages of the war, the Messerschmitt 110 equipped the backbone of the German night-fighter force. The aircraft illustrated was flown by Oberleutnant Wilhelm Johnen of II./NJG 5 early in 1944; note the cumbersome assembly of aerials on the nose, carried by some Messerschmitt 110s until improved equipment became available. (via Aders)

79. This aircraft being readied for flight, unusually, has two long-barrelled 20mm MG 151 cannon with flash eliminators in the upper nose position, in place of the normal MG 108 30mm cannon. (via Seeley)

80, 81. During the final year of the war, Messerschmitt 110 night-fighters fell easy prey to the US escort fighters roaming over Germany by day and, at night, they were equally vulnerable to the Mosquitoes of the RAF's No. 100 group.

80▲ 81▼

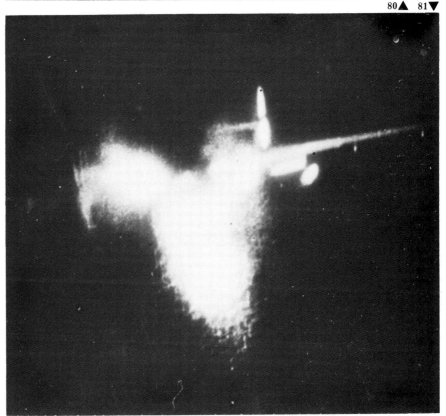

▲82 ▼83

82–85. Trial installations fitted to FW 190s. **82.** Six MG 151 20mm cannon, for the bomber-destroyer rôle. **83.** An underwing mounting for an MK 103 30mm high velocity cannon, for the ground-attack rôle. **84.** Modified to carry the SB 1000, with the lower fin removed to give sufficient ground clearance. **85.** Modified to carry the Blohm und Voss 246 Hagelkorn unpowered glider-bomb.

84▲ 85▼

86, 87. Close-ups of the nose of a Ju 188A-3 torpedo bomber, operated by III./KG 26. The nose aerials belong to the FuG 200 Hohentwiel search radar. The underwing racks for the torpedoes, and the bulge running down the starboard side of the fuselage housing the torpedo mechanism, can be clearly seen.

88. Inside the cockpit of a Ju 188A-3, showing the basic flying instruments in front of the pilot and the radar indicator in front of the observer.

87▲ 88▼

◀86

▲89

▲90

▲91 ▼92

89–92. Experiments with rigidly-towed stores. 89, 90. A Heinkel 177 undergoing trials with a rigidly-towed fuel tank, complete with its own wing and under-carriage. A similar system (91, 92) was fitted to the Messerschmitt 262 fighter-bomber, for the carriage of an SC 500 bomb. Although such systems underwent extensive trials, German aircraft never flew in action with rigidly-towed stores.

93, 94. Reconnaissance aircraft. **93.** A Dornier 217M of the little-known Aufklärungsgruppe Nacht (identification letters K7), photographed at Copenhagen in 1945. **94.** Messerschmitt 109s of a short-range reconnaissance unit, indicated by the letters on the rear fuselage in contrast to the numbers carried by aircraft of single-engined fighter units. Probably, these are the G-8 sub-type, which carried a single, vertical camera in the fuselage behind the cockpit, and the sole armament of one cannon which was fired through the airscrew spinner.

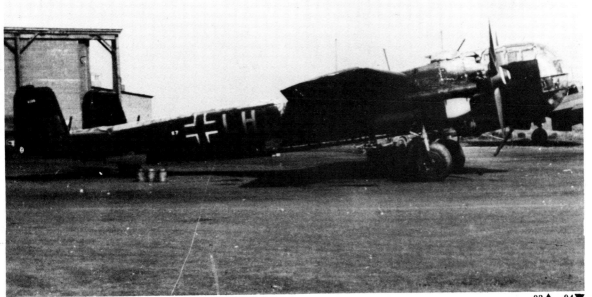

93▲ 94▼

me 410

▲95 ▼96

95-97. Messerschmitt 410 bomber-destroyers of II./ZG 76, pictured in the summer of 1944 when the unit operated from Königsburg-Neumark. At this time the main armament of these aircraft comprised a pair of MK 103 30mm high-velocity cannon in the lower part of the nose. (Schob)

97▼

98. Focke Wulf 190A-8 of IV. (Sturm) JG 3, which operated from Schongau in the summer of 1944. The heavily armoured Sturmgruppe aircraft suffered heavy losses in aircraft destroyed and damaged, so much so that there was often insufficient time to paint unit markings on to newly delivered aircraft before they went into action. (Romm)

99, 100. Features of the FW 190A-8. **99.** A close-up of the wing installation for the MK 108 30mm cannon. **100.** The laminated glass panel on the side of the canopy to afford the pilot increased protection. Visible at the bottom of the photograph is the additional armour plate on the side of the fuselage, mounted externally.

101. An unusually-painted Messerschmitt 109G-14 belonging to III./JG 3, the unit which often flew as escort for the IVth (Sturm) Gruppe. (Romm)

100▲ 101▼

▲102

102. Arado 234B jet bombers of 9./KG 76, photographed at Burg near Magdeburg late in 1944 when the unit was working up to go into action. (KG 76 Archive)

103–109. Scenes at Burg near Magdeburg as 9./KG 76 prepares for action with its new Ar 234Bs. **103.** Major Hans-Georg Bätcher, the commander of III./KG 76. **104.** A line-up of Ar 234s.

103▲   104▼

▲105

▲106 ▼107

105, 106. Bätcher climbing into his Arado and strapping into his seat. **107.** A Kettenrad half-track used to tow an Arado into position **108.** On other occasions standard service lorries were used. **109.** A pair of concrete practice bombs can just be seen on the bomb rack fitted under the starboard engine of this aircraft. (KG 76 Archive)

108▲ 109▼

▲110

▲111 ▼112

110. In the summer of 1944 the long-nosed FW 190D entered service. The radial-type cowling tended to conceal the fact that this aircraft was powered by the Jumo 213 in-line liquid-cooled engine. Here, a brand new FW 190D-9 is awaiting delivery. (Romm)

111–114. This selection of photographs comes from the collection of ex-Oberleutnant Oskar-Walther Romm. All the aircraft depicted are FW 190Ds of Stab IV./JG 3 at Prenslau in March 1945. Romm (**113**) was commander of this unit, and his personal aircraft (**114**) carried Gruppe commander's chevrons on the fuselage.

113▲ 114▼

▲115 ▼116

115, 116. The Tank 152, developed from the FW 190D and one of the highest performance piston-engined fighters built, was on the point of going into large-scale service when the war ended.

117, 118. After the war, captured German aircraft were test-flown by many of the victorious nations. This Messerschmitt 163 was modified in the Soviet Union as a two-seat trainer; so far as is known it was not flown on rocket power. (via Geust)

117▲ 118▼

119, 120. Work on the DFS 346 swept-wing rocket-powered high-speed research aircraft had not progressed far when Germany surrendered. After the war the incomplete aircraft and those working on it were moved to Podberezhye in the USSR, where the machine was completed. During 1946 the aircraft underwent unpowered flight tests from Toplistan airfield near Moscow, carried aloft by one of the ex-USAAF B-29s which landed in the USSR towards the end of the war. Rocket-powered flights followed and there is evidence that the DFS 346 was the aircraft the Russians claimed to have flown faster than sound in May 1947, some five months before Captain Chuck Yeager of the USAF exceeded Mach 1 in the Bell XS-1 rocket aircraft. (via Geust)